PRAY FOR HER

Pray for Her

*30 days of breakthrough prayer
for the woman you love*

Amanda Hayhurst

Published 2025
Printed in the United States of America

31 30 29 28 27 26 25   1 2 3 4 5 6 7

ISBN 979-8-9910019-3-9

All Biblical references will be in ESV
unless otherwise noted.

Contents

Acknowledgments

My husband already knows how deeply I appreciate his vulnerability for the sake of others' healing. This time around, I also want to thank two incredible women who brought this book to life behind the scenes—my editor, Lauren Sanchez, and my book designer, Lydia Hall. Thank you for being the creative geniuses you are and for pouring so much heart into every detail. Your gifts are felt on every page.

Introduction

Early in my relationship with my husband, Marcus, I was a complete mess— I'll admit it. I brought more baggage into that relationship than I could carry, and truthfully, so did he. We both walked in with unresolved issues we didn't even know we had until they started spilling out. After we got married, my husband quickly felt the weight of these unresolved issues and his natural response was to jump into 'fix it' mode—because that's what you do when something's broken, right? But it didn't take long for us to realize that no matter how hard we tried, we couldn't fix each other. And maybe that wasn't our job in the first place.

When we adopt a "fix-it" mentality toward someone else's problems, our boundaries can easily blur. Without even realizing it, we might start carrying our partner's burdens simply because we long to see change so desperately. Do you find yourself absorbing the weight of your partner's bad day as if it's your responsibility to make it better? Or maybe you feel pressured to resolve her spiritual struggles, as if they're yours to fix? The truth is, we are not called to fix or control—it's not our role. What we really need to do is shift our focus from **fix and control** to **surrender and prayer**.

If you are reading this book, chances are you want more for the woman you love. Perhaps it's your wife, and you're longing for her to put God first in her life, or maybe it's your girlfriend or fiancé, and you're desperate to see a breakthrough in a particular area of her life. Whatever change you are longing to see, know that God is more than able, and you can find rest knowing the weight of change is not yours to carry.

If you were sitting across the table from my husband, he would tell you he's a man of solutions. It's how he's wired. When I share something difficult, his instinct isn't to empathize or listen—it's to fix. Here's a classic example:

> Me: *"Ugh. I think my friend is upset with me. She hasn't responded to my texts all day. I mean, maybe she's just busy . . . but what if she's mad? Did I say something wrong? I keep replaying our last conversation, and now I'm convinced I did something. It's me. It's totally me."*

> Him: *"Sooo, call her?"*

And that's it! I pour my heart out with fifty-one words of emotion, and he responds with three words of logic. This is how our communication usually goes. Sound familiar? Where I lean into the story, the feelings, and the nuances, he cuts straight to the chase with a practical, no-frills solution.

Although my husband's intentions are always to help—*and honestly, his solutions are usually spot on* (but don't tell him I said that)—sometimes, what we need most isn't a fix. We need someone to simply listen, to sit with us in the hard moments, and ultimately, to cover us in prayer. And the best person to pray for us are the men God gave us . . . *You.*

You have the most power in prayer where God has given you the most authority. In other words, the areas of your life where he's entrusted you with influence are the very places where your prayers carry the greatest weight and impact. No one can pray for the woman you love like you can. All that worry and discontent in your relationship should be fuel for your prayer life. Think about it like raising the sail on a boat; you can't control the wind or make it blow harder, but you can set the sail to catch it. In the same way, your desire for change is meant to push you to prayer, where God then moves to guide you and your partner in the way he wants you to go.

What Does Prayer Actually Do?

Prayer is a privilege we have to approach God in an intimate conversation, one that can include praise, repentance, thanksgiving, and intercession. It's something we do with great boldness as Hebrews 4:16 reminds us, "Let us then *with confidence (boldness)* draw near to the throne of grace, that we may receive mercy and find grace to help in time of need." Because we have a Great High Priest, Jesus Christ, interceding on our behalf, we can confidently approach God's throne at any time, in any place, and *he will help us.*

Prayer is also an ongoing act of surrender:

A surrender of your partner's future into God's capable hands.
A surrender of your will for God's will.

A surrender of your frustration for God's supernatural peace.

A surrender of your doubts and skepticism for an unshakable trust in God and his plan (both for you and your partner).

Surrendering in prayer isn't about giving up; it's about letting go of what was never yours to hold and acknowledging that while you deeply love your partner, God loves her even more. He knows her needs, struggles, and heart better than you ever could. Your role isn't to fix her or to be her savior—that's God's job. Your role is to stand in the gap, intercede, and trust that the same God working in your life is also working in hers.

And here's the beauty of it: prayer doesn't just change the person you're praying for—it changes you. As you consistently intercede on her behalf, you'll find your own heart softening, your perspective shifting, and your faith deepening. The burdens you once carried alone will begin to feel lighter as you allow God to take them from you, one day at a time. Over time, you'll start to see glimpses of how he's working behind the scenes, crafting something more beautiful than you could ever imagine, and in those moments, you'll realize that surrender isn't weakness— it's the strongest, most loving thing you can do.

As a man, you're likely a visual thinker, someone who processes and retains information best when you can see it clearly. In my previous book, *Pray for Him*, I included a simple graphic to help women remember what their role was, and wasn't, as they prayed for the men they love. I realized it would be just as helpful to include that here for you!

While praying for Marcus, I jotted this down on a piece of paper as a visual reminder for myself. It served as a powerful anchor, helping me stay focused on what my job was and what God's job was. My hope is that it does the same for you.

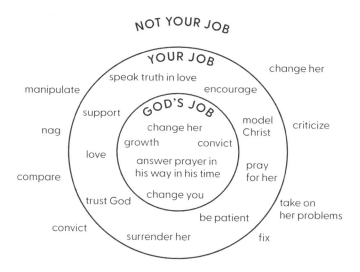

When we truly understand the difference between our role and God's, it brings a profound sense of peace—peace that comes from trusting him with our partner's future. But it doesn't stop there. This shift transforms how we interact with our partner. We let go of nagging, taking on all their problems, criticizing, fixing, comparing, and even manipulating—often without realizing we were doing it in the first place. I can confidently say that both my husband and I felt a deep sense of relief when we released this weight of change that was never ours to carry.

Does Praying Specifically Really Matter?

Like I said at the beginning of this introduction, I brought suitcases full of baggage into my relationship with Marcus. Being in a relationship really has a way of exposing those parts of ourselves we'd rather keep hidden, and there were countless moments when I gave him reasons to throw in the towel. After polling other women, I found we wrestle with struggles that can manifest similarly in our relationships. Maybe you've noticed some of these same patterns in the life of your partner:

- Constant nagging and need for reassurance
- Resorting to the silent treatment or avoiding conflict
- Setting unclear or unspoken expectations
- Rehashing past issues during present conflicts
- Comparing you to other men
- Overloading your schedules without room for connection
- Overlooking your stress or dismissing your struggles

No one wants their loved one treating them this way—my husband certainly didn't, and if we're being honest, there were days when walking away felt like the easier option. But the truth is, no relationship is free from struggles. We live in a broken world, and as a result, are broken people. Oftentimes, that brokenness can become glaring in the context of a deeply committed relationship.

The reality is that there is always a deeper story behind the behaviors we see in ourselves and our partners. In your partner's life, something may have happened—

something she experienced or even something she did—that caused her to believe a lie from the Enemy. For example, if she experienced betrayal by someone she trusted, she might have internalized the lie, *I am unworthy of love.* That belief could lead her to avoid conflict out of fear of rejection or upsetting others. Or perhaps she endured trauma, such as physical or emotional abuse, leading her to accept the lie, *I am damaged,* or *Something is wrong with me.* This could result in behaviors that appear needy, such as seeking constant reassurance from you, stemming from insecurities she may still be wrestling with deep inside.

This is why it's so important to pray over the root issues affecting the ones we love. As this devotional guides you to do, you'll learn to pray over deep wounds—like trauma, generational chains, and the lies of the Enemy. It also helps you see your partner through God's eyes as you learn to untangle her behavior from her identity because your eyes are more open to what's behind it.

I love the assurance that prayer gives us as we pray over specific areas in our partner's life. We develop a tough type of God-confidence because we have released every aspect of our partner's life into the capable hands of the Lord. 1 John 5:14 reads, "And this is the confidence we have toward him, that if we ask anything according to his will, he hears us." It goes on to read, "And if we know that he hears us in whatever we ask, we know that we have the requests that we have asked of him" (1 Jn. 5:15).

See, consistent and specific prayer builds unwavering contentment and peace in our hearts because we learn to trust God . . . *with everything.* Philippians 4:6–7 commands us, "Do not be anxious about anything, *but in everything*, by prayer and petition, with thanksgiving, present your requests to God. And the peace of God, which transcends all understanding, will guard your hearts and your minds in Christ Jesus." What a promise! Who doesn't want their heart and mind guarded with God's perfect peace?

My husband has shared with me that he often struggles to find the right words when it comes to praying for me. He'll walk into his office, sit down at his desk, and open his Bible to read Scripture—something he could do for hours. But when it comes time to pray over me, the words don't always come. That's one of the reasons I wrote this devotional. I wanted to provide him, and other men like him, with the prayers that women so desperately need.

This devotional is filled with powerful breakthrough prayers for nearly every area of your partner's life. But like I warned the women in *Pray for Him*, I must also warn you: this isn't just about her. God is about to do a transformative work in *your own heart*. And honestly, since you are the man and spiritual leader, it is imperative that God do a work in your heart. Because you still carry around your sinful flesh, your heart is tainted with control, pride, bitterness, unforgiveness, and hidden sins that God must deal with first. I pray that you lead by example in your own life with every prayer you pray over her life.

You'll notice a journal page included after each daily prayer. And yes, I get it—you're a strong, burly man, and here I am asking you to journal. But stick with me! While pre-written prayers are a great starting point, it's important to leave space for the Holy Spirit to guide you. As you pray, you might feel prompted to go off-script and pour your heart out about something else entirely—and that's okay! Prayer is simply an intimate conversation between you and your Heavenly Father. God already knows what's on your heart, but he wants *you* to share it with him in your own words. Use the journal page to capture those thoughts, prayers, and any reflections over the next thirty days. It's a chance to deepen your connection with God and open your heart to what he wants to do in your life and the life of the woman you love.

Lastly, in case you don't hear it directly from your partner, I just want to take a moment to say *thank you*. Thank you for committing to pray for her. Thank you for standing in the gap and staying the course, even when throwing in the towel and walking away feels easier. In the words of John Maxwell, "Everything worthwhile is uphill." And prayer is no exception–prayers that can feel like an uphill battle against doubt, frustration, and weariness. In those uphill moments, ask God for the strength to keep going because remember—*no one can pray for her like you can*. There is something extraordinary, fulfilling, healed, and whole on the other side of your prayers.

BEFORE YOU BEGIN:
PRAYING FOR YOU

Your Own Heart

Remember, this prayer journey is not just about the woman you love. You are embarking on a journey that will transform your own heart, too. And honestly, that is the greatest witness for Christ you can have in your relationship. As your partner sees you becoming more transformed into the image of Christ, she will want what you have. In fact, it will be one of the most attractive things about you. As I've grown older, I've realized that my husband's physical appearance matters less to me than the state of his heart. I find him most attractive when he's showing kindness, immersing himself in God's Word, and spending time in prayer. The way he seeks God is more endearing than any outward quality ever could be. So, as you pray for the heart of the woman in your life, don't forget to pray for your own heart, too. This journey is about both of you growing closer to God and each other.

Dear God,

As I begin this journey of praying over _____, I ask that you show me the state of my own heart. Search me and know my heart, test me and know my anxious thoughts (Ps. 139:23), and reveal any hidden sins in me (Ps. 19:12). God, I repent of _____(name your sins specifically) and receive your mercy, grace, and forgiveness today. As I pray for transformation in my partner's life, I pray you would shape me into the man you've created me to be. Guide me to live in a way that is noticeable to her and draws her closer to you. Help me to be like King David, a man after your heart—in constant pursuit of you. Use the discontentment I feel in my relationship as fuel for my prayer life. As much as I am praying for specific breakthrough, teach me how to just sit before you and receive your love, patience, mercy, forgiveness, and grace. I recognize that I cannot give my partner what I haven't first received from you. Help me to extend to her the same love, patience, mercy, forgiveness, and grace that you show me each day. As you form me more into the image of your Son, help me to model that same sacrificial love Christ gives me to her.

In Jesus' name, Amen.

"Search me, O God, and know my heart! Try me and know my thoughts! And see if there be any grievous way in me, and lead me in the way everlasting."

Ps. 139:23–24

DAILY PRAYER JOURNAL

Date:

Learning to Trust

As a man, you've likely felt the weight of being in control—of your life, your circumstances, and maybe even, at times, the life of your partner. It's such a heavy burden, and letting go of that control can feel unnatural and risky. Oftentimes, the path forward isn't clear and doesn't make sense but that's exactly where trust comes in. The truth is—God has a plan for your life and your partners, and that plan is the very best plan. The more you pray and surrender your partner to the Lord, the more assurance and peace you will experience. Remember, prayer is just a continual surrendering of your will for the Lord's, and the will of the Lord can always be trusted, both for you and the woman you love. Even Jesus had to pray in the Garden of Gethsemane, "Not my will, Lord, but your will be done" (Lk. 22:42). Let his example encourage you to trust that God's plan and the timing of his plan is always better.

Dear God,

Today I choose to trust you with _____'s future. I recognize that you are the Creator of all things, the Author of life, and the One who holds my partner's future securely in your hands. Yet, Lord, I confess that there are times when I try to carry burdens that aren't mine to carry. Forgive me for the moments I've held on too tightly, thinking I know what's best. Teach me to release control and place my partner fully into your care. Help me to remember that you love her more than I ever could, and your plans for her are far greater than anything I could imagine. Give me the faith to trust in your timing, even when it doesn't align with mine, and to believe that your ways are always higher and better. Fill my heart with peace and contentment when I feel the urge to fix, control, or carry things that belong to you. Form me into a man of prayer, faithfully lifting her up to you every single day. Jesus, you showed us what it means to trust completely when you prayed, "Not my will, but yours be done." Help me to follow your example, surrendering my desires and my fears into the hands of my good and capable Father. Thank you for always being trustworthy.

In Jesus' name, Amen.

"*Father, if you are willing, remove this cup from me. Nevertheless, not my will, but yours, be done.*"

Lk. 22:42

7

DAILY PRAYER JOURNAL

Date: _____

Eyes to See

Have you ever noticed how parents see things in their children that no one else does? My son could hold up a drawing that looks like a complete mess to everyone else, but to me, it's a masterpiece—an early glimpse into the heart and creativity of a budding artist. I see past the mess to the potential and the beauty that others may overlook. In the same way, God calls us to see our partners—not just for who they are in the moment, but for who he has created them to be. The woman you love bears the very image of God, even in moments when her behavior doesn't necessarily reflect it. At times, it may be easier to focus on the flaws, the imperfections, and the quirks that drive you crazy but God sees her heart. He sees the potential, the unique beauty he has woven into her. When you can learn to look beyond the surface to see her as God does, you can love her more deeply and truly appreciate her for the beautiful, imperfect master-piece she is.

Dear God,

You have created human beings in your image as the pinnacle of your creation. Today, I ask that you help me see _____ the way you do. You have created her in your very likeness—full of value and purpose. I pray you would cultivate in me a heart of gratitude for how you have uniquely wired her, and to praise her for those things that make her who she is. Help me to look past the imperfections and the flaws, especially in moments of frustration, and to see the beauty and potential you have placed within her. Give me eyes of grace, compassion, and understanding and teach me to love her with the same unconditional love that you give me every day. When she stumbles and struggles, remind me to be a source of encouragement to her, and not judgment. Give me the ability to speak the truth in love. When the Enemy tries to tempt me to dwell on the negative, give me a Godly perspective, full of hope for my partner's future. Thank you for the blessing that she is in my life and for how you have uniquely created her.

In Jesus' name, Amen.

"For the Lord sees not as man sees: man looks on the outward appearance, but the Lord looks on the heart."

1 Sam. 16:7b

DAILY PRAYER JOURNAL

Date:

THE HEART OF THE MATTER: PRAYING FOR HER

God First

If one prayer trumps them all, it would be for the woman you love to make God first in her life. It truly is the foundation of all the others and a prayer that can be the most difficult to see breakthrough. We are living during a time when we are completely overstimulated with a million things fighting for our attention. This means that we must be even more intentional in fighting against distractions in our spiritual lives. The Enemy knows exactly how to target your partner's weaknesses, tempting her heart to drift from her relationship with the Lord to lesser things. Things he knows will never truly satisfy her. Perhaps it's excessive indulging in entertainment like social media, worrying about finances, or focusing too much on her physical appearance. Whatever it is— God's simple promise remains true: Seek me and my Kingdom above all else and I will give you everything you need (Matt. 6:33). This beautiful promise comes with just one requirement: that we put God first.

Dear God,

More than anything else, I long for _____ to seek you first in every aspect of her life. Draw her closer to you in ways that only you can do and remind her of your promise that you will provide for all of her needs when

15

she seeks you first (Matt. 6:33). I know that the Enemy has a plan to keep her from pursuing you, so I pray for your protection over her right now in the name of Jesus Christ. Strengthen her in moments of temptation when she is distracted by the things of this world that try to steal her focus away from you. I pray she would have a hunger for your Word, a passion for prayer, and a desire to follow you wholeheartedly. When life feels overwhelming, remind her that you are her refuge and strength, her ever-present help in trouble (Ps. 46:1). I also ask that you would help me to encourage her in her pursuit of you. May I live in a way that stirs her affections for you and inspires her to draw near to you. Thank you for being a God who wants to spend time with us in the first place.

In Jesus' name, Amen.

"But seek first the kingdom of God and his righteousness, and all these things will be added to you."

Matt. 6:33

DAILY PRAYER JOURNAL

Date:

Spiritual Growth

For years, I felt stuck in my walk with God. Sure, Marcus and I went to church and prayed before meals, but a deep, flourishing relationship with the Lord? I just wasn't there yet. I still wasn't consistent in reading God's Word or faithful in spending time with Him in prayer. Honestly, I was still a baby Christian even though I technically had been a Christian for many, many years. Much like the believers were described in Hebrews 5:12–14, I was reliant on milk when I should have been eating solid food. Unfortunately, this is all too common for many of us. We grow spiritually apathetic and become comfortable with living a mediocre spiritual life. But the truth is, God wants so much more for his children. Maybe your partner is in a similar place. Maybe she's stopped praying regularly, no longer prioritizes quiet time with the Lord, avoids Christian community, or leans more on self-help than Scripture. Whatever the case, God is inviting her to step into the abundant life he's promised—to stop settling for less when he is offering so much more.

Dear God,

Thank you for always desiring more for us and making a fulfilling, abundant life with you possible. I pray that

_____ would grow in her walk with you and that she would be discontent with a surface-level, stagnant kind of faith. Give her the desire to be in your Word every single day and to know you in ways she never has. Make the stories and truths of Scripture come alive and become so real to her, keeping her hungry for more. Help her to develop spiritual habits that keep her consistently growing in her relationship with you, like going to Church, reading your Word, and spending time with you in prayer. Give her the boldness to be public with her relationship with you—sharing her testimony with others and looking for ways to glorify you. I pray that the Holy Spirit would empower her to walk in your ways, to discern your voice, and to grow in the fruits of the Spirit. May she be a woman who exemplifies you in all she does. I also ask that you help us to grow closer together as we both grow closer to you.

In Jesus' name, Amen.

"For though by this time you ought to be teachers, you need someone to teach you again the basic principles of the oracles of God. You need milk, not solid food, for everyone who lives on milk is unskilled in the Word of righteousness, since he is a child. But solid food is for the mature, for those who have their powers of discernment trained by constant practice to distinguish good from evil."

Heb. 5:12–14

DAILY PRAYER JOURNAL

Date: _____

Body Image

Spend just five minutes on social media, and you'll likely encounter perfectly curated images of women whose beauty seems almost impossible to attain. Research suggests that nearly 88% of women compare themselves to these images, often leaving them feeling dissatisfied with their own appearance. For the woman you love, this comparison trap can lead to low self-esteem, depression, an unhealthy relationship with food, and difficulty embracing her natural beauty. In a culture that idolizes external beauty, it's crucial for her to anchor her confidence in the truth of who God says she is—his masterpiece, fearfully and wonderfully made in his image. She is loved, valued, and worthy, not because of how she looks, but because she is uniquely and beautifully created in the very image of God himself. In addition to praying, you can help her anchor her identity in this truth by intentionally recognizing and affirming her inner beauty—the qualities of her heart that God values most.

Dear God,

Thank you for the incredible gift of _____ and for placing her in my life. She is fearfully and wonderfully made, created in your very image with significant value and worth. Please help her to see herself through your eyes—as your handiwork, created with significant love and purpose. Protect her heart and mind from the lies of this world—that she must meet certain standards of beauty to be accepted or valued. When she is tempted to compare herself to others, guard her thoughts, replacing any lies with your truth: that her worth is not determined by her appearance. Help her to find unshakable confidence in the knowledge that she is your beloved daughter, not in the reflection in the mirror. Give her the strength to reject society's standards of beauty and to embrace her body as the beautiful temple you have given her—a body that allows her to love, serve, and glorify you. Lord, teach me to affirm her inner beauty—how she treats others, her kindness, her character, her humility and her pursuit of you. Thank you for how you have uniquely created her to reflect your image and for loving her more deeply than I ever could.

In Jesus' name, Amen.

"Do not let your adorning be external—the braiding of hair and the putting on of gold jewelry, or the clothing you wear— but let your adorning be the hidden person of the heart with the imperishable beauty of a gentle and quiet spirit, which in God's sight is very precious."

1 Pet. 3:3–4

DAILY PRAYER JOURNAL

Date:

Coping Mechanisms

So often, we turn to physical solutions to fix our emotional and mental problems. In the Ancient Near East, God's people repeatedly abandoned his glory in favor of what they could see and touch—carving images of animals or false gods in search of comfort and control. They exchanged the living God for lifeless creations. Today, your partner may not be shaping idols out of stone, but when stress hits, she might reach for distractions—like wine, shopping, or endless Netflix—to cope. While those things may bring temporary relief, they can't satisfy the deep ache of her soul. Only God offers lasting comfort. It's in his presence and through his Word that we find the peace our hearts crave when life feels overwhelming. Healthy outlets aren't wrong, but when they replace intimacy with God, they become modern-day idols. That's why the very first commandment God gave was, "You shall have no other gods before me" (Exodus 20:3). Only he can fully satisfy, fully heal, and provide what this world never can.

Dear God,

You are the Great Comforter and the only thing that truly satisfies. I lift up _____ to you today, knowing you see her struggles, her pains, and the way she copes with the challenges of life. Father, give her wisdom to recognize the ways she may be turning to temporary solutions or unhealthy patterns, and help her replace those by sitting in your healing presence and reading your Word. Teach her to lean on you first and to find her greatest satisfaction in you alone. Give her the courage to feel the hard things and to process her feelings, drawing even closer to you in those moments. Help her find healthy ways to decompress like staying physically active, spending time with friends, cooking, and journaling. May she find comfort knowing that because you created her and know her intimately, you are able to give her heart what it needs the moment she needs it most. Help me be a source of encouragement for her and a safe place she can turn to in difficult times. Give me the wisdom to understand her struggles, the patience to walk alongside her, and the ability to always point her back to you.

In Jesus' name, Amen.

"You shall have no other gods before me."

Ex. 20:3

DAILY PRAYER JOURNAL

Date: _____

_____

_____

_____

_____

_____

_____

_____

_____

_____

_____

_____

_____

_____

_____

_____

_____

_____

_____

_____

_____

_____

_____

_____

_____

_____

_____

Her Purpose

One of the most profound questions we ask ourselves as we step into adulthood is, *"What is my purpose?"* For a long time, I wrestled with that question. I had a successful career in medical sales, but it didn't feel purposeful. After becoming a mom, I began to see more meaning in my day-to-day, but something still felt unsettled. Eventually, God shifted my path—drawing me out of the corporate world and into a calling to write and encourage others. Looking back, I now see that I was living out my purpose all along—first as a wife, then as a mother, and even in the hard, hidden seasons of caring for a sick child. Purpose isn't always flashy or public. It's often quiet, sacred work that shapes us. And as we grow sensitive to the whispers of the Holy Spirit, we begin to hear His *calling*—those specific invitations that require our full yes. As you pray for your partner, trust that even now, God is at work in her—equipping her for the next step, and reminding her that her life carries deep, God-given purpose in every season.

Dear God,

Thank you for the calling you have placed on _____'s life. You have created her uniquely—with gifts, talents, and a purpose that only she can fulfill. I pray that she earnestly seeks your will for her life through daily prayer and time in your Word. As she's seeking your direction, may you generously pour out your wisdom, just as you promise in James 1:5. Reveal to her the plans you've already written for her, plans to prosper her, and give her hope and a future. I pray you would quiet any fears or doubts she may have about her future, and that she would learn to trust you completely. Open her eyes to the opportunities you've placed in front of her and give her the courage to step through those doors. Help her to see how her unique experiences, talents, and challenges are all being woven together for a greater purpose. Fill her heart with peace, knowing that she doesn't have to figure it all out on her own because you are with her. Refine her in times of preparation, forming her more into the image of your Son, Jesus. May she find joy in knowing that her identity and purpose are rooted in you, not in her achievements or circumstances.

In Jesus' name, Amen.

"For we are his workmanship, created in Christ Jesus for good works, which God prepared beforehand, that we should walk in them."

Eph. 2:10

DAILY PRAYER JOURNAL

Date:

Setting Healthy Boundaries

If there's one area where many women collectively struggle, it's setting healthy boundaries, and it's why so many are having important conversations about how to do it effectively. Boundaries are not just practical—they are essential for emotional, spiritual, and relational health. If your partner struggles with boundaries, you may notice she often says "yes" when she really wants to say "no" or she may avoid difficult conversations because she dislikes conflict or fears disappointing others. Over time, this can leave her feeling exhausted, overwhelmed, and maybe even resentful. The weight of carrying too much can dim the joy she once had, but there is good news! God invites us to walk in freedom, not burnout. The woman you love doesn't have to live in a constant state of feeling stretched beyond her limits. As she learns to protect her peace, she will grow more present in her relationship with the Lord and with you.

Dear God,

Thank you for the gift of _____ and the way you've uniquely created her to love and serve others. Help her to know that her worth is not found in how much she does for others but in simply being your beloved daughter. Remind her that it is not selfish to guard her heart and protect her peace but a reflection of trusting you. Give her courage to say "no" when it's necessary, and clarity to recognize the things that are not hers to carry. As she does this, remove any false guilt she may feel in her effort to set boundaries. Help her find freedom in surrendering the weight of over-commitment and discover the peace that comes from walking in the center of your will. Gently remind her that her goal in life is to please you and not man, becoming a servant of Christ in all she does. Lord, teach me to honor her boundaries and lead with wisdom, grace, and love. Let our relationship reflect the harmony and peace that come from respecting these healthy limits. I pray that as she continues to grow in this area, she will draw closer to you, experience greater joy, and find renewed strength in your presence.

In Jesus' name, Amen.

"For am I now seeking the approval of man, or of God? Or am I trying to please man? If I were still trying to please man, I would not be a servant of Christ."

Gal 1:10

DAILY PRAYER JOURNAL

Date: _____

Godly Community

For the woman you love, building a circle of girlfriends to share life with might not seem all that challenging. She may have friends from the gym, the neighborhood, or even old high school or college pals. But just like so many other women out there, she may struggle with finding relationships where she can truly be her full, authentic self. What she really longs for is a deeper kind of connection—a community that moves beyond surface-level talk. She needs friends who are edifying, deeply intimate, and uplifting, always pointing her back to Jesus in every season of life. These kinds of friendships aren't just meaningful—they're transformative. Imagine the gift of her being part of a godly community—a safe space where she can remove her mask, be completely herself, share her struggles, and reach out for help when she needs it most. It's these special women that will be the extra support she needs as God is transforming her into the woman he created her to be.

Dear God,

I know the gift of godly friendships could be in _____'s life. I lift her up to you today, asking that you surround her with godly women who are full of love, grace, and truth—women who will encourage her, build her up, and walk alongside her in every season. May they be friends who point her back to you, who pray for her, and who love her unconditionally. Lord, create a safe and sacred space for her to be vulnerable, to share her struggles, and to grow deeper in her faith through community. If these women are within a local Church, I pray she would have the courage to seek out this community through small groups and other social gatherings. Help her to feel seen, known, and loved, both by you and by those you place in her life. If there are any women in her life who are toxic or drawing her further from you, I pray you will give her the wisdom to create healthy boundaries and even remove friendships when necessary. When she does feel alone or discouraged, remind her that you are her constant companion, the One who never leaves or forsakes her.

In Jesus' name, Amen.

"Iron sharpens iron, and one man sharpens another."

Prov. 27:17

DAILY PRAYER JOURNAL

Date:

Breaking Generational Chains

That area you are desperate for your partner to experience a breakthrough might be more deeply rooted than you think. It could have been passed down through generations—a pattern woven into her family's history. Maybe she struggles with avoiding conflict, reacting in anger, or being habitually critical of others, you, or even herself. These could be the same struggles her mother faced, and her mother before her. It's these deeply ingrained patterns that can sometimes feel hopeless with thoughts like, *This is just the way I am,* or *I'll never change.* But those thoughts are lies straight from the Enemy's mouth, designed to keep her bound. For years, I believed I would always struggle with the same unhealthy coping mechanisms. Turning to substances to ease the sting of a hard day—wine, in my case—felt inevitable, because it was a generational pattern in our family. But God, in his infinite power and love, stepped in and freed me. And the same God who worked in me can work in the life of the woman you love.

Dear God,

You are all powerful and there is no generational sin too strong for you to break. I pray for the struggles _____ faces, acknowledging that some of these patterns may

36

have been passed down through generations before her—patterns of _____ (name them if you know them). Although she may feel powerless to overcome these generational chains, they are no match for your redeeming power. You are the God who breaks every chain, who redeems what was lost, and who restores what was stolen. Oh God, break the generational chains that have held her and her family captive. Where there has been conflict, bring healing. Where there has been anger, sow gentleness. Where there has been shame, remind her of her identity as your beloved daughter. Lord, I ask that you dismantle every lie of the Enemy that tells her she is bound to her past or destined to repeat it. Remind her that through Christ, she is a new creation—the old has gone, and the new has come. Father, I trust you to do what only you can do. Restore what has been broken in her life and family line. May her life be a testimony of your grace and redemption, a light for others to see your glory.

In Jesus' name, Amen.

"Is not this the fast that I choose: to loose the bonds of wickedness, to undo the straps of the yoke, to let the oppressed go free, and to break every yoke?"

Isa. 58:6

DAILY PRAYER JOURNAL

Date: _____

Self-esteem

Growing up, there was a girl I greatly admired in school named Lindsey. It wasn't just because of her striking beauty and loads of friends, but the way she was so unapologetically herself. She was comfortable in her own skin, and quite frankly, I wasn't. I doubted myself and struggled to find my voice. I wonder now—looking back—if her parents poured into her identity, affirming over and over who God said she was. The truth is that lasting confidence comes from having a proper view of who God is and who we are. Everything your partner does will flow from this foundation. God loves her deeply and has incredible plans for her life. He calls her his daughter, bought with a price, his beautiful handiwork, created to do the good works he prepared in advance for her to do. This kind of God-centered confidence will root itself deeply in her soul, shaping her understanding of who she is, why she's here, and where she's going.

Dear God,

Thank you for placing _____ in my life and creating her with such care, purpose, and love. Help her to see herself through your eyes—as your beloved daughter, chosen, cherished, and called. Regardless of what this world says, teach her that her worth is not found in her

39

appearance, achievements, or what others think of her, but in the unchanging truth that she was bought with a price and is fearfully and wonderfully made. Cultivate habits in her life that increase her daily knowledge of these truths and not the lies from this world. Plant the truths of your Word deeply in her soul—giving her the confidence that comes from knowing she is your handiwork, created for good works that you prepared for her long before she was born. I pray against any lies from the Enemy that would seek to steal her joy or make her doubt her identity in you. Replace any lies with your unfailing promises. May she walk boldly in the plans you have for her, secure in the knowledge that she is loved, valued, and created for a purpose. Help me to encourage and affirm her inward beauty daily, reminding her of who you say she is.

In Jesus' name, Amen.

"I praise you, for I am fearfully and wonderfully made. Wonderful are your works; my soul knows it very well."

Ps. 139:14

DAILY PRAYER JOURNAL

Date:

Overcoming Anxiety

There are times I may be physically present but mentally I'm on a train to Panicville. Perhaps the woman you love struggles with similar thoughts: *Is this symptom serious? Why hasn't she texted me back? How will I get all this done?* Living in this state of anxiety is exhausting and oftentimes, we arrive here when we worry about what we do not know. What a gift it is to be fully present—not just physically but mentally and emotionally. This is why Philippians 4:8 commands us to, "*think on what is true.*" The verse goes on to tell us to set our minds on things that are honorable, just, pure, lovely, etc., but let's stop right at the word *true*. "To think on what is *true*." When your partner anchors her mind in truth—what is real and present today, not the fears of tomorrow—she can stop anxiety in its tracks. And even on those days she gets rerouted to Panicville, she does have a weapon-*Prayer*. Prayer is the medium that exchanges our worry and anxiety for God's supernatural peace–a peace that comes right in and interrupts our present-day worries. A peace that is the byproduct of prayer.

Dear God,

Thank you for making perfect peace possible for your children, something we can't accomplish on our own.

42

I lift _____ up to you today and the anxiety and worry she carries. Protect her heart and mind with your perfect peace. When her thoughts race to worst-case and what-if scenarios, remind her of the truth found in your Word. Help her to focus on what is true, honorable, just, pure, lovely, and praiseworthy. Help her to recognize when her thoughts are veering toward fear or panic, and give her the strength to redirect them. Let your truth anchor her heart and quiet her anxious thoughts. Teach her to continually bring her worries to you in prayer, trusting that you care for her and will meet her every need. As she brings her burdens to you, I pray that your supernatural peace that surpasses all understanding would flood her heart and mind in the name of Jesus Christ. Remind her that she is not alone, and she does not have to carry her burdens by herself. Thank you, Lord, for being her refuge, her strength, and her ever-present help in trouble. May your peace fill her heart and mind today and every day.

In Jesus' name, Amen.

"*Do not be anxious about anything, but in everything by prayer and supplication with thanksgiving let your requests be made known to God. And the peace of God, which surpasses all understanding, will guard your hearts and your minds in Christ Jesus.*"

Phil. 4:6–7

DAILY PRAYER JOURNAL

Date: _____

Healing from Shame

From the beginning, the Enemy wasted no time using one of his most powerful weapons to keep us from stepping into who God created us to be: *shame*. When Adam and Eve ate the forbidden fruit, their first instinct wasn't to repent—it was to hide. When they heard God walking in the garden, they withdrew in fear (Gen. 3:8), and that's exactly what shame does. It isolates. It convinces us that we are defined by our worst moments. It makes us uncomfortable in our own skin, whispering lies over our identity. For the woman you love, there may be wounds from her past—shame she still carries, and insecurities that run deep. Shame wants to keep her trapped there, but *God doesn't call us to hide—he calls us to draw near.* Through Jesus, shame has no claim on her. His death and resurrection didn't just pay for her sins—they shattered the weight of shame itself. She is forgiven. She is redeemed. She is covered in *grace upon grace*. And THAT is the Gospel truth that changes everything.

Dear God,

Thank you for the freedom we have in your Son, Jesus Christ. You see the burdens _____ carries today—the wounds that linger, and the shame that tries to keep her bound. But I know that shame has no place in the life of

45

a daughter of the King. Jesus, you came to set the captives free. You took not just our sin but our shame to the cross, declaring once and for all that we are made new in you. I pray that my partner would no longer listen to the lies of the Enemy that tell her she is unworthy, unlovable, or defined by her past. Instead, let her hear your voice—the voice of truth—calling her *redeemed*, *forgiven*, and *set free*. Lord, replace every whisper of shame with the power of your Word. When she is tempted to hide, remind her of Hebrews 4:16—that she can boldly approach your throne of grace and receive mercy in her time of need. When insecurities creep in, remind her that she is fearfully and wonderfully made (Ps. 139:14). And when she doubts her worth, remind her that she was bought with a price—the precious blood of Christ (1 Cor. 6:20). Give me wisdom to speak words that build her up, patience to walk alongside her, and a heart that continually prays for her.

In Jesus' name, Amen.

"Let us then with confidence draw near to the throne of grace, that we may receive mercy and find grace to help in time of need."

Heb. 4:16

DAILY PRAYER JOURNAL

Date:

Sexual Purity

When it comes to sexual purity, many typically associate that with a younger crowd, but do not be fooled. Sexual purity is a mental and physical struggle for many adults that often stems from some form of unmet need or neglect in their past. For me, this struggle was rooted in a complicated relationship with my dad, leaving a void in my soul that craved love and affirmation. The problem is, when these things are not received from a godly source, it leaves room for the Enemy to creep in, distorting our view of intimacy. What begins as a search for some sort of affirmation can lead to compromises we never intended. But know this: No amount of love or affection can fill a heart that is designed to first be filled by God. True security isn't found in being noticed—it's found in knowing you are already chosen. Jesus sees your partner, knows her, and calls her worthy. As a man of God, you must intercede for the woman you love—praying for her healing, speaking life over her, and reminding her she doesn't need to chase approval when she is already cherished by her perfect Father in Heaven.

Dear God,

I come before you today, lifting up _____ into your hands. You formed her, know her, and call her your beloved daughter. Lord, you see every longing in her heart—the deep desire to be loved, seen, and affirmed. And I know that no earthly attention can satisfy the worth you have already placed within her. Father, I pray for her healing. Where wounds from the past have left her searching for validation, let your love be her anchor. Where insecurities try to whisper lies, let your truth be her shield. Remind her that she is already chosen, already loved, already enough in you. Guard her heart, Lord. Strengthen her against the pressures of this world that try to redefine beauty, worth, and love. Let her identity be rooted in you, not in fleeting attention or empty affirmations. Fill every space where she feels unseen with the unshakable truth that you see her, you cherish her, and you delight in her. Help me, as the man who loves her, to speak life over her. Let my words reflect your truth and let my actions mirror your grace. May I love her with purity, honor her with respect, and always point her back to you—the source of her ultimate worth. Thank you, Jesus, for the gift of her life. Continue your good work in her heart, drawing her closer to you every day.

In Jesus' name, Amen.

"For this is the will of God, your sanctification: that you abstain from sexual immorality; that each one of you know how to control his own body in holiness and honor, not in the passion of lust like the Gentiles who do not know God."

1 Thess. 4:3–5

DAILY PRAYER JOURNAL

Date: _____

Resisting Temptation

Don't you wish following Jesus meant the Enemy would finally leave us alone? Unfortunately, I think the opposite is sometimes true—we have an even bigger target on our backs. But thankfully, God doesn't leave us to our own devices. For the times we find ourselves at our most tempted, he has provided a way out: *prayer*. Scripture commands us to draw near to the throne of grace for help and he will provide an escape (Heb. 4:16). I don't know what your partner struggles with, but no temptation is too much that the Lord can't provide a way out. Perhaps it's a habit she can't seem to break, reacting in her anger, or an unhealthy relationship that needs to be cut off, whatever it is—she can have the victory. Even Jesus himself was tempted in the wilderness, yet through the power of the Holy Spirit, he was not overcome by it and that same Holy Spirit can empower the woman you love. Temptation is real, but so is his victory.

Dear God,

Thank you for placing _____ in my life. I lift her up to you today, asking for you to protect her from the Enemy's schemes to derail her. You know where she is weakest and the temptations she faces that threaten to deter her from the path you've set before her. But I know that no temptation has overcome her that is not common to man and you will always provide a way for her to endure it. When she feels weak, remind her that you are her refuge. When she feels trapped, show her the way out. When the Enemy whispers lies, let your truth drown them out. Fill her heart with wisdom to recognize temptation, strength to resist it, and the confidence to stand firm in who you've created her to be. Oh, Holy Spirit—be her guide. Just as you sustained Jesus in the wilderness, sustain her. Guard her mind, protect her heart, and lead her in the way everlasting. Give her victory over anything that tries to steal her peace, her joy, and her identity in you. And Lord, please help me to cover her in prayer daily, to be a source of encouragement, and to stand beside her as she walks in your freedom.

In Jesus' name, Amen.

"No temptation has overtaken you that is not common to man. God is faithful, and he will not let you be tempted beyond your ability, but with the temptation he will also provide the way of escape, that you may be able to endure it."

1 Cor. 10:13

DAILY PRAYER JOURNAL

Date: _____

Honesty and Openness

Nothing can unravel a relationship more quickly than a lack of trust. Without trust, doubt creeps in, communication weakens, and emotional distance grows. It's hard to feel truly close to someone when you're constantly questioning their words or motives. In any relationship, the level of intimacy is always dependent on the level of honesty. Without honesty, there can be no true connection, and for your partner to be vulnerable, she needs to feel safe, valued, and heard. If she struggles to open up, fear may be holding her back. She may worry about being misunderstood, judged, or dismissed. Your role isn't to pressure her into honesty but to create an environment where honesty feels safe. The more tender-hearted, trustworthy, and patient you are, the more she will feel secure enough to share her heart. Add in praying for her, and you will begin to see her walls crumble, your communication grow, and your trust deepen. When you cover her in prayer, you invite God into the spaces to do what you can't and what only he can.

Dear God,

Thank you for always being a safe place where we can fully be ourselves and be fully known. I pray _____ would feel safe in our relationship and that it would be built on a foundation of honesty, openness, and security. Lord, you see the fears, wounds, and past experiences that may make it hard for her to be fully vulnerable. You know the things she holds inside, the burdens she carries, and the walls she has built to protect herself. I pray you would fill her heart with peace—reminding her that she is deeply loved, fully known, and completely safe in your arms. Give her a heart that rejoices in truth, and the courage to speak the truth in all circumstances. Help me to be a reflection of your love, offering patience when she hesitates, grace when she struggles, and a listening ear when she needs to be heard. Let my words bring life and encouragement, not pressure or judgment. Teach me to love her in a way that makes room for healing, growth, and a deeper connection between us. Most of all, I surrender our relationship to you. Help us to walk in honesty, grace, and faithfulness, trusting that you are always at work in us.

In Jesus' name, Amen.

"Do not lie to one another, seeing that you have put off the old self with its practices and have put on the new self, which is being renewed in knowledge after the image of its creator."

Col. 3:9–10

DAILY PRAYER JOURNAL

Date: _____

Heart of Humility

Have you noticed how our culture constantly pits men and women against each other? It has become an endless tug-of-war over who holds more power, who is more right, and who should take the lead. But at the core of this tension, we don't just see differing opinions; what we see is pride. The truth is—it was never meant to be a competition. In a world that celebrates self-promotion and dominance, humility often takes a backseat but God calls his childrens to something far greater. Humility isn't about thinking less of ourselves; it's about surrendering our need to be right, to win, and to control. It's about laying down pride and choosing love, even when it's hard. This is especially true in relationships. Many arguments in my marriage could have been avoided had we stopped trying to always be right and instead embraced humility. When we choose to humble ourselves, we don't just have better relationships—we reflect Christ, who humbled himself to the point of death, all for love.

Dear God,

Thank you for the incredible woman you have placed in my life. I lift _____ up to you today, asking that you shape her heart to reflect the humility of Christ.

In a world that promotes pride, competition, and self-promotion, teach her to live humbly—glorifying you. Give her confidence in who she is as your daughter so that she doesn't feel the need to prove her worth or fight for control. Lord, I pray that she would be quick to listen, slow to speak, and slow to anger. Soften her heart to let go of the need to be right and instead choose love, even when it's hard. Help her to trust that humility is not weakness but the very posture of strength, grace, and wisdom. When conflict arises, remind her that true victory is not in winning arguments but in honoring you. May she seek to build others up instead of elevating herself. Just as Jesus humbled himself, even to the point of death, teach her to walk in the same spirit of grace and selflessness. Help our relationship to reflect your love—built on a foundation of humility, patience, and a heart willing to serve.

In Jesus' name, Amen.

"Do nothing from selfish ambition or conceit, but in humility count others more significant than yourselves."

Phil. 2:3

DAILY PRAYER JOURNAL

Date:

Dealing with Conflict

If your partner is anything like me, she may struggle with conflict—not just dealing with it, but avoiding it at all costs. Some women grew up learning to confront it head-on, eager to resolve issues quickly, while others were conditioned to always try to keep the peace, even if it meant ignoring their own needs. On the flipside, there are those who address conflict head-on, but it often ends in explosive emotions rather than resolution. However she's wired, the goal remains the same: to work through it with each other, not against each other. One of the greatest gifts you can give her is your *understanding*. When my husband Marcus and I have taken the time to listen first, our empathy toward one another grows. Conflict isn't just about what happened—it's often about why it happened. Like we discussed earlier in this devotional, there's usually something deeper beneath the surface, and when we are patient enough to seek the why behind the what, we begin to see one another the way God does—and that changes everything.

Dear God,

Thank you for the gift of relationships and for the gift of _____ in my life. Fill her heart with peace, wisdom, and humility in the moments when conflict arises. Help her to navigate these situations with grace and strength— not from a place of fear, pride, or defensiveness—but with a heart that seeks understanding and unity. Lord, your Word says that a gentle answer turns away wrath (Proverbs 15:1). Help her to speak with kindness, even in frustration, and to listen with an open heart. If past hurts or fears cause her to withdraw or react in ways that don't reflect who you created her to be, I pray you would heal those wounds in the name of Jesus Christ. Continually teach her how to resolve conflict in a way that honors you. Above all, I pray she leans on you as her source of wisdom and discernment, responding not as the world does but how the Holy Spirit does—in love, joy, peace, forbearance, kindness, goodness, faithfulness, gentleness, and self-control. I pray we draw closer to one another as we both honor you in how we deal with the conflict in our lives and in our relationship.

In Jesus' name, Amen.

"*Know this, my beloved brothers: let every person be quick to hear, slow to speak, slow to anger; for the anger of man does not produce the righteousness of God.*"

Js. 1:19–20

DAILY PRAYER JOURNAL

Date: _____

_____

_____

_____

_____

_____

_____

_____

_____

_____

_____

_____

_____

_____

_____

_____

_____

_____

_____

_____

_____

_____

_____

_____

Discipline

Don't you wish we could make progress without the setbacks? Maybe you were finally in a groove—hitting the gym consistently—then you got sick and lost your momentum. Or maybe you committed to waking up early, spending time with the Lord, and reading your Bible every morning, only to miss a few days and feel like you're back at square one. Typically, it's not starting something that's difficult; it's continuing to do it day in and day out, even when you don't *feel like* doing it. This reminds me of the apostle Paul. Despite so many obstacles—imprisonment, beatings, literal shipwrecks, and betrayals—he continued to pursue his calling. It was John Maxwell who once said, "Everything worthwhile is uphill." Whatever the Lord has called your partner to do, it will be difficult. But with God's help, it is more than possible. She can remain steadfast. And your prayers are one way to help her do just that.

Dear God,

Thank you for enabling us to do the things you've called us to do—to have the most fulfilling and purpose-filled life. Thank you for the calling you have placed on _____'s life, and her desire to walk in obedience to you. Lord, I know how discouraging setbacks can be. When

63

the obstacles come—when exhaustion, doubt, or frustration try to pull her away from the good work you've started in her—please strengthen her. When she struggles to stay consistent, fill her with perseverance. Just as the apostle Paul pressed on despite trials, I pray she will continue moving forward, not in her own strength, but in yours. Your Word says in Galatians 6:9, *"Let us not grow weary in doing good, for at the proper time we will reap a harvest if we do not give up."* Help her to trust in that promise—that every step she takes, even the ones that feel small or insignificant, are leading to something greater. Father, when she feels weak, be her strength. When she feels discouraged, be her hope. When she is tempted to quit, remind her of the purpose you have set before her. And Lord, help me to be a source of encouragement and support—to pray for her, to lift her up, and to remind her that with you, all things are possible.

In Jesus' name, Amen.

"Let us not grow weary of doing good, for in due season we will reap, if we do not give up."

Gal. 6:9

DAILY PRAYER JOURNAL

Date: _____

Mental Health

I met a friend at Chick-fil-A the other day to catch up, and during our conversation she shared how defeated she was feeling. She was completely overwhelmed—like there were a million tabs open in her brain. So many of us feel this way, and I think I may know why: *we are completely overstimulated*. So many things fight for our attention—our phones, schedules, responsibilities, and relationships. We rarely give ourselves permission to slow down. Stillness feels unnatural because busyness has become our default. But when our calendars are packed to the brim, it can cause us to feel anxious, discontent, and exhausted. It really does take a toll on our mental health. Maybe that's why God doesn't just *recommend* rest—he *commands* it. In Psalm 46:10, we are reminded: *"Be still, and know that I am God."* Stillness isn't passive—it's an act of trust, a declaration that God is in control, not us. Pray today that your partner will find peace in the stillness, knowing that it's God himself who holds all things together.

Dear God,

Thank you for the gift of our minds and for the peace and stillness you offer us. You have designed _____ to not live in constant overwhelm but to rest in your perfect peace. Guard her heart and mind against any plan of the Enemy to cause chaos. You see the weight she carries— the racing thoughts, the anxious moments, the mental exhaustion that can sometimes feel overwhelming. In a world that constantly pulls at her attention, I pray that you would quiet the noise and bring stillness to her soul. Your Word says in Psalm 46:10, *"Be still, and know that I am God."* Help her to release the burdens she was never meant to carry. When stress, fear, or self-doubt try to take hold, remind her that you are her refuge, her strength, and her ever-present help (Ps. 46:1). Lord, renew her mind daily. Replace anxious thoughts with your truth. Fill her heart with peace that surpasses all understanding (Phil. 4:7). When she feels overwhelmed, be her anchor. Help her rest in the truth that her mental health is not just a battle to fight but a space where you desire to bring healing and restoration.

In Jesus' name, Amen.

"Come to me, all who labor and are heavy laden, and I will give you rest. Take my yoke upon you, and learn from me, for I am gentle and lowly in heart, and you will find rest for your souls. For my yoke is easy, and my burden is light."

Matt. 11:28–30

DAILY PRAYER JOURNAL

Date: _____

Physical Health

Why is getting healthy so hard to do but so easy to lose? My husband has always struggled to keep his weight in check. I once convinced him to try the Whole 30 diet, and by the end of those thirty days, I thought we might need marriage counseling. It was hard work—finding the right ingredients, sticking to a meal plan, resisting the intense sugar cravings. And before we knew it, we had regressed right back to our old habits. Just like that, Marcus put the weight back on. Sometimes, we have control—choosing what we eat and staying active. But other times, we don't—an unexpected diagnosis or a hereditary illness. The truth is—where we *do* have control, we are called to honor God with our bodies (1 Cor. 6:19–20). It is possible for the woman in your life to steward her health well and in the areas beyond her control, to rest in God's sovereignty and grace.

Dear God,

Thank you for making our bodies in your image and for commanding us to steward them well. I lift _____ up to you today, asking for your hand to be over her physical health. You created her body with care, and you know every detail of her well-being. Help her to honor you with her body—not out of guilt or pressure, but out of gratitude for the life you've given her. Give her wisdom and discipline in making healthy choices, and remind her that her worth is not found in a number on a scale but in being your beloved daughter. Use me to encourage her—both with my words and by my actions—in both eating well and remaining physically active. For the things beyond her control—sickness, fatigue, hereditary conditions—I plead for your healing in the name of Jesus Christ. May every ache and pain be a reminder to draw closer to you, Lord, so you can comfort and satisfy her like nothing else can. I pray she finds rest in your sovereignty, knowing that you hold her in your capable hands.

In Jesus' name, Amen.

"Or do you not know that your body is a temple of the Holy Spirit within you, whom you have from God? You are not your own, for you were bought with a price. So glorify God in your body."

1 Cor. 6:19–20

DAILY PRAYER JOURNAL

Date:

Comparison

If there's anything that makes it hard to resist comparison, it's social media. Just as God can use anything for our good, the Enemy can use it for our detriment. For years, I found myself comparing my husband to other men. *Why can't Marcus spiritually lead like that guy? Why doesn't he affirm me like my friend's husband does?* Comparison is a trap—we always measure our worst to someone's best, leaving us discontent and dissatisfied. Maybe you don't even realize how subtly the Enemy tempts you to compare your partner to the women you see. *Sarah cooks for her husband every night—why doesn't mine? Emily is the picture of submission—why does mine cringe at the thought?* But here's the truth: any energy spent comparing is wasted energy. Instead of measuring her against someone else, pray for her. Ask God to shape her into the woman he's called her to be—and to shape you into the man he's created you to be. We aren't called to compare. We're called to love, to honor, and to lift each other up to the Lord.

Dear God,

Thank you that you do not compare us to one another but instead, you see us individually and are so very patient with us. I confess that I have allowed comparison to creep into my heart at times, measuring my relationship against unrealistic expectations shaped by social media, culture, and pride. Lord, forgive us where we have looked outward instead of trusting your unique plan for our growth. I ask that you guard _____'s heart against comparison, especially when the world tempts her to see what others have rather than the blessings you've given her. When the Enemy tries to shift our focus to what we lack, remind us to fix our eyes on you and what you are doing in our own relationship. Thank you for the unique and beautiful way you have made my partner. Help me to honor, cherish, and love her as Christ loves the Church. Replace comparison with gratitude, criticism with encouragement, and envy with contentment. Lord, refine us. Shape us into a couple who builds one another up—not just in words, but in prayer, in love, and in grace.

In Jesus' name, Amen.

"*A tranquil heart gives life to the flesh, but envy makes the bones rot.*"

Prov. 14:30

DAILY PRAYER JOURNAL

Date: _____

_____
_____
_____
_____
_____
_____
_____
_____
_____
_____
_____
_____
_____
_____
_____
_____
_____
_____
_____
_____
_____
_____
_____
_____
_____
_____
_____

Emotional Health

I'm sure there have been moments in your relationship where you've thought, "I love this woman, but she is acting crazy right now!" I get it. Emotions can be unpredictable and sometimes all over the place, but they aren't bad, just misunderstood. In fact, they are a gift from God—he himself experiences emotions, and since we are made in his image, we do too. But as Lysa TerKeurst wisely says, *"Feelings are indicators, not dictators."* They alert us that something needs attention, but they don't always lead us to the truth. For example, we may *feel* like God is angry with us when hardships come, but Scripture tells us that trials are part of living in a broken world. Jesus Himself said, "In this world you will have trouble. But take heart! I have overcome the world" (Jn. 16:33). When your partner learns to take her emotions to Scripture and measure them against God's truth, she will find His supernatural comfort. And as Jesus says, "The truth will set you free" (Jn. 8:32).

Dear God,

Thank you for creating _____ in your image, with the ability to feel deeply and love fully. I know that emotions are a gift from you, but I also know how overwhelming they can be at times. Lord, when she feels anxious, discouraged, or uncertain, remind her that her emotions do not define her—Your truth does. Help her to see that her feelings are not the enemy but indicators pointing her to what she needs. Teach her to turn to your Word as her source of truth, rather than being led by temporary emotions. Remind her that she can feel her emotions deeply while also glorifying you with her reactions. May she be slow to speak and slow to become angry, modeling the self-control that you make possible for all who indwell the Holy Spirit. When she feels unseen, remind her that you are near. When she feels overwhelmed, fill her with your peace. When she feels unworthy, whisper to her heart that she is chosen, and loved. Teach me to be a safe space for her emotions, to listen well, encourage often, and pray over her daily. When her emotions feel chaotic, help me to remain calm and to be a constant source of truth and stability.

In Jesus' name, Amen.

"Trust in the Lord with all your heart, and do not lean on your own understanding. In all your ways acknowledge him, and he will make straight your paths."

Prov. 3:5–6

DAILY PRAYER JOURNAL

Date:

A Servant Heart

I wonder how many arguments Marcus and I could have avoided if we had simply chosen to put each other first. One morning, something clicked for me—instead of expecting a 50/50 effort, I decided to give 100. I started with the small things. When I made breakfast, I gave him the best, crispiest pieces of bacon. When we argued over something insignificant, I chose to let it go first. And you know what? He noticed. Suddenly, he was serving me too—cleaning my car when it was filthy, jumping in to help with the kids when he saw I was exhausted. We fell into a rhythm of serving each other, not out of obligation but out of love. Jesus Himself modeled this kind of servant-hearted love, saying, "For even the Son of Man came not to be served but to serve, and to give his life as a ransom for many" (Mk. 10:45). When the woman you love puts humility over pride and service over self, your relationship will flourish. Love grows strongest when it's built on selfless giving, not on keeping score.

Dear God,

Thank you for the example of your Son who did not come to be served, but to serve. Shape _____'s heart to reflect this same servant-hearted love. Help her to not just show love with her words, but with actions of humility, kindness, and selflessness. Where there is any hidden pride or entitlement, expose it and replace it with a desire to consider others more significant than herself, looking not only to her own interests but to the interests of others (Phil. 2:3–4). Teach us both to love like you do—to put each other's needs before our own, to show patience when we want to prove a point, and to lead with grace rather than pride. When my partner wants to keep score, remind her that true love isn't just about what we receive, but what we give. Help her to find opportunities to serve others in our community, at church, and in our family. Bless our relationship with a spirit of humility and mutual service. May we strive to outlove, outserve, and outgive one another—not for recognition, but because that's how you love us. Grow us in unity, strengthen our bond, and help us reflect your love in everything we do.

In Jesus' name, Amen.

"*Do nothing from selfish ambition or conceit, but in humility count others more significant than yourselves. Let each of you look not only to his own interests, but also to the interests of others.*"

Phil. 2:3–4

DAILY PRAYER JOURNAL

Date: _____

Growing in Wisdom

Don't you wish we didn't have to learn things the hard way? I look back on choices I made–the ones that weren't God's best for me–and wonder how much pain I could have avoided. My mom shared with me how her choices led to heartbreak; I knew what the bible had to say about my decisions, and deep down, I even knew better. But just because we have wisdom available doesn't mean we always apply it. King Solomon is the perfect example of this. He was the wisest man to ever live, yet he disobeyed God by marrying foreign wives who led him into idolatry (1 Kings 11:1–11). His downfall wasn't a lack of wisdom—it was failing to apply what he knew. The truth is, we don't have to learn everything the hard way. God places people in our lives to guide us, gives us his Word for direction, and the Holy Spirit to convict and lead us. Pray today that the woman you love not only seeks God's wisdom—but that she walks in it. Because peace isn't found in just *knowing* the right thing—it's found in *living* it.

Dear God,

Thank you that the fear of the Lord is the beginning of wisdom, and that true wisdom comes from you alone. Fill _____ with Godly wisdom, keen discernment, and supernatural understanding. You have given us your Word to guide us, your Spirit to lead us, and godly people to counsel us. I pray that she turns to these gifts from you and not the world as she seeks direction in every decision she makes. Help her to recognize the difference between what feels right in the moment and what is truly best for her life. Guard her from decisions that could lead to regret, and instead, shape her heart to desire what is good, holy, and pleasing to you. Father, don't just give her wisdom—give her the courage to apply it. Build a rhythm in her life where she prays continuously about the decisions she's making so she can be sensitive to the leading of the Holy Spirit. Help her to trust that your ways are higher, your timing is perfect, and that obeying you will always lead to peace, purpose, and joy.

In Jesus' name, Amen.

"If any of you lacks wisdom, let him ask God, who gives generously to all without reproach, and it will be given him."

Js. 1:5

DAILY PRAYER JOURNAL

Date: _____

Motherhood

I'm not sure what your relationship was like with your mom, but whether it was amazing or *a little complicated*, I know this—it shaped you. Our parents have the power to love us like no one else can and, at times, frustrate us like no one else can. Pouring into the next generation is a huge responsibility. As parents, we can model God's love—a love that is sacrificial, unconditional, and sometimes requires superhuman patience (especially when the kids won't listen, won't sleep, and have somehow lost their shoes ... *again*). Thankfully, God doesn't leave us to figure it out alone. The woman you love can turn to his Word for wisdom and other godly women for guidance. If her own upbringing was challenging, God can heal those wounds and show her how to be a mother after his own heart—one whose children respect and honor her. Whether she's already a mother or plans to be one day, her greatest impact won't come from being perfect, but from pointing her kids to the perfect love of God.

Dear God,

Thank you for being the perfect Father and for loving us more than anyone else can. I pray you would equip _____ with wisdom, strength, and grace as she nurtures and guides the next generation. Shape her into a woman after your own heart—one who loves, leads, and teaches with patience and grace. Lord, remind her that she doesn't have to do this alone—that you are with her in every moment, from the joyful milestones to the overwhelming days. Help her to turn to your Word and godly community for wisdom in parenting well. Teach her to reflect your love in the way she speaks, disciplines, and cares for those entrusted to her. If there are any wounds from her own childhood, I pray for your healing and restoration and that she may parent from a place of wholeness, not hurt. Would she learn to first be a daughter to the perfect Father, so she can give her children the same love, patience, and grace that you so generously give her. Help her to find joy in the sacred role of motherhood, and help me to always be her encourager, her supporter, and her partner in raising a family that honors you.

In Jesus' name, Amen.

"As a father shows compassion to his children, so the Lord shows compassion to those who fear him."

Psa. 103:13

85

DAILY PRAYER JOURNAL

Date: _____

Priorities

As I mentioned earlier in this devotional, the hinge pin of all the prayers you pray over your partner is that she puts God first. When he is at the center, everything else—work, friendships, family, hobbies—falls into its rightful place. Solomon reminds us in Ecclesiastes that we are to enjoy these things as gifts from God, not as substitutes for him. Perhaps the woman in your life is prioritizing things that aren't gifts from God at all but are actually hurting her. If that's the case, your prayers can be a catalyst for conviction—the gentle nudge she needs to surrender what is not of God and realign her heart with his purpose. Pray that she embraces those things that shape her into the woman God created her to be—serving others, nurturing relationships, stewarding her health, and walking in wisdom. When God's desires for her life become her desires, she will be anchored in what truly matters.

Dear God,

Thank you for designing our lives to be the most satisfying and fulfilling when we seek you first. Teach _____ to seek you first in all things, knowing that when you are at the center, everything else falls into its rightful place. Help her find joy in the good gifts you have given—her

87

relationships, her work, her health—but never allow those things to take your place on the throne of her heart. If she is investing time or energy in things that are not from you, bring gentle conviction. Help her to surrender anything that is leading her away from your best, and replace it with pursuits that bring her closer to you—serving others, nurturing relationships, growing in wisdom, and stewarding her health and mind. Lord, let her be a woman of purpose, rooted in your truth, unwavering in faith, and walking confidently in the path you have set before her. Strengthen her heart, renew her mind, and fill her with a peace that surpasses all understanding. May she always delight in you, trusting that when her desires align with yours, she will flourish in every area of her life.

In Jesus' name, Amen.

"Commit your work to the Lord, and your plans will be established."

Prov. 16:3

DAILY PRAYER JOURNAL

Date:

Father Wounds

If you've ever met someone and thought, *This girl has daddy issues*, I was her. I never wanted to be that girl—the one who craved a man's attention to feel worthy—but I was every bit of her. What we often call "daddy issues" are really father wounds, deep imprints left by the relationship with our earthly fathers. And for good reason. Out of all the ways God could have chosen to relate to us, he chose fatherhood–a sacrificial, unwavering love where he adopts us as his own, leads us with wisdom, and never fails us. If the woman you love wrestles with deep insecurity, an excessive need for affirmation, or a constant search for validation, she may be carrying hidden father wounds. But here's the good news: healing is possible. She may need to learn, maybe for the first time, what it truly means to be a daughter—loved by a perfect Father who is always present, always faithful, slow to anger, and never breaks his promises. Because when she embraces his love, she'll no longer chase after lesser versions of it.

Dear God,

Thank you for being the perfect father and for calling us your children. You know the depths of _____'s heart– the places that have been wounded, the hurts she may not even have words for. You see every moment she has felt unseen, unloved, or unworthy. And we acknowledge that it's only one who can truly heal her. Heal the places in her heart that have been shaped by the absence, neglect, or brokenness of her earthly father. Where rejection has left scars, pour out your unfailing love. Where disappointment has planted fear, replace it with trust in your goodness. Where insecurity has taken root, remind her that she is fearfully and wonderfully made, fully known, and deeply loved by you. Help her to see you as her perfect Father—always present, always faithful, never distant or dismissive. Show her that she doesn't have to strive for love or chase after validation because in you, she already has all the acceptance she will ever need. Break the chains of any false beliefs that tell her she is unlovable or unworthy, and help her walk in the confidence of being your beloved daughter. Give me wisdom to love her well, to point her back to you, and to be patient as you do the healing work in her heart.

In Jesus' name, Amen.

"Father of the fatherless and protector of widows is God in his holy habitation."

Psa. 68:5

DAILY PRAYER JOURNAL

Date: _____

_____
_____
_____
_____
_____
_____
_____
_____
_____
_____
_____
_____
_____
_____
_____
_____
_____
_____
_____
_____
_____
_____
_____
_____
_____

Her Love for You

Have you ever watched a rom-com (probably against your will) and thought, *This is completely unrealistic?* The grand, dramatic gestures—like holding a boombox outside her window or chasing her through an airport—somehow erase every problem in the relationship. If only love were that simple! In reality, love isn't about a single sweeping moment—it's about the small, consistent choices made every day. It's not always easy, and it's certainly not always glamorous. The fairy tale we see on screen isn't real life. And honestly? God's definition of love is *so much better*. Love, as God designed it, is patient and kind, it rejoices in truth, it's not driven by fleeting emotions or perfect timing but by sacrificial commitment—a love that mirrors the love we receive from the Father. When your partner loves you in this way, she's not just loving you—she's reflecting the divine, unshakable love of God Himself. And that's not just romantic; that's holy. It's a love worth fighting for.

Dear God,

Thank you for loving us so sacrificially, so much so that you sent your Son Jesus to die for our sins so we could be saved. I know that true love—the kind that reflects your very heart—is not based on fleeting emotions or grand

gestures but on patience, kindness, and truth. I pray
_____ receives your love first so that she may pour out
that love in the way she speaks, acts, and cares for those
around her—including me. Help her love be patient
and steadfast, even in difficult moments. Teach her to
show grace and forgiveness just like you so graciously
do. Even when it's difficult, give her the courage to speak
the truth in love so our relationship can be edifying and
honoring to you. Protect her heart from the world's lies
about love—based on fleeting feelings and not on a loving commitment. As she draws closer to you, continue
to conform her more into the image of your Son, Jesus.
And Lord, help me to love her the same way—as Jesus
loves his Church—with humility, selflessness, and a servant's heart. May our love story be one that continually
honors you.

In Jesus' name, Amen.

*"Love is patient and kind; love does not envy or boast; it is not
arrogant or rude. It does not insist on its own way; it is not
irritable or resentful; it does not rejoice at wrongdoing, but rejoices with the truth. Love bears all things, believes all things,
hopes all things, endures all things."*

1 Cor. 13:4–7

DAILY PRAYER JOURNAL

Date:

Conclusion

What an accomplishment, friend! You've just spent thirty days praying for the woman you love. That is no small feat. There are a million other things you could have been doing, yet you made a commitment because you believe your prayers matter. And they absolutely do. No one knows your partner the way you do, which means no one else can intercede for her quite like you can. Every time you get on your knees to pray for her, you're doing something far greater than you may realize—you are releasing control and embracing God's plan. You're learning, day by day, to trust God with her future, to let go of your own expectations—believing his ways are higher and his timing is perfect. Keep praying. Keep trusting. God is still working in ways you cannot see.

But I do need to warn you: You may experience, as time goes on, that discouragement creeps in. Maybe you don't see the breakthrough as quickly as you'd hoped, or maybe the Enemy whispers that God isn't so faithful after all. But please remember this: Your job is not to change her, convict her, or control the timing of her growth. Everyone's spiritual journey is different. God's plan for each person unfolds in his perfect way and his perfect time. What you do have—the unshakable assurance of prayer—is more powerful than you realize. We know that if we ask anything according to God's will, he hears us. And if he hears whatever we ask, we can trust that he is working—giving us what is best for us right now (1 Jn. 5:14–15). God is faithful to give your partner exactly what she needs today, tomorrow, next week, this year. *Only he knows what is best for her right now.* Your role is to pray for her, encourage her, and love her as Christ loves the Church. Remember what Scripture teaches about love:

> *"Love is patient and kind; love does not envy or boast; it is not arrogant or rude. It does not insist on its own way; it is not irritable or resentful; it does not rejoice at wrongdoing, but rejoices with the truth. Love bears all things, believes all things, hopes all things, endures all things." (1 Cor. 13:4–7)*

Try reading this passage again, but this time, replace the word *love* with your own name. Let it challenge you. Let it convict you. Are you patient? Are you kind? Are you quick to forgive and slow to anger? This simple exercise is a powerful way to hold yourself accountable to the kind of sacrificial love God calls you to in your relationship. Because real love—God's love—isn't about feelings or convenience. It's a daily choice–a commitment to love selflessly, consistently, and unconditionally, just as Christ loves us.

As you continue praying for her, I encourage you to surround yourself with godly men: brothers in Christ who genuinely want what's best for you and your relationship. When you feel weary, invite them into your prayers. There is power in praying together. James knew this well, so he was sure to remind us: *Confess your sins to one another and pray for one another, that you may be healed"* (Js. 5:16).

Early on in my marriage, I remember uttering to one of my closest friends, "I just feel like my husband will never change. I honestly think I may end up leaving him." But after hearing me out, my friend looked me straight in the eyes and said, "I'm sorry, but I won't let you." She knew the ins and outs of my marriage. She knew it was a relationship God had called me to, and so she prayed with me. She fought for me, for our relationship. She spurred me on.

Thank God we don't have to do this alone. Maybe you gather a group of men and go through this devotional together, or maybe you return to these prayers often—praying the same one day after day. That's okay. I know I certainly have. And let me tell you, I have seen God show up and do miraculous things. Friend, this journey isn't just about her heart—it's about yours, too. The more you draw near to God in prayer, the more you will be conformed to the image of Christ. And I promise you this: the woman you love will take notice because the way you live your life is the greatest testimony you will ever share. Keep praying. Keep believing. The best is yet to come.

Made in United States
Orlando, FL
08 June 2025

61773734R00066